Roellen Brown

Some Deaths in the Delta

A National Council on the Arts
Award Selection

Some Deaths
in the Delta

and other poems

ROSELLEN BROWN

The University of Massachusetts Press

Some of these poems have appeared in the following
magazines and anthologies, whose editors are thanked
for permission to reprint: *Antioch Review, Apple,
Approach, Arts in Society, Atlantic Monthly, Chelsea,
Choice, Denver Quarterly, Massachusetts Review,
The Nation, New Orleans Review, New South,
North American Review, Northwest Review, The Seventies,
Sumac, University Review, Best Poems of 1965* (Borestone
Mountain Awards), *Black and White in American
Culture* (University of Massachusetts Press),
Campfires of the Resistance (Bobbs-Merrill).

The opening lines of "The Bedouin Said (When
Asked)" are quoted by Daniel Lerner in *The
Passing of Traditional Society* (The Free Press
of Glencoe)

For Marv, the poems between the lines

Contents

III. CAN'T REMEMBER
     WHAT I MEANT BY HOME

I.
The Delta

Landing in Jackson (1964)

I wear my fear like wool against the skin,
walking from corner to corner of this graceless city,
squinting down doorways, warily at faces.
For a familiar token I take the sky,
stretched taut between the tent-poles of my sight—
that northern blue that bore me up for hours,
then set me gently down in this ungentle place.

What shame may be here keeps its uneven heartbeat
under the breast-pocket, the clean white hanky;
if any danger passes, it keeps its eyes
turned in like something hidden in the palm.
I sniff from corner to corner, guilelessly,
skulking for welcome.

Living in Opposition
for H.B.W.

A walking life.
No one is welcome
going the long way between safety and safety.

*

Martyrs decide on death too soon,
slip out of their skin and leave it anywhere it drops.
Soul's underwear.
They like to drown swallowing blood
heads up, bones dry, always polite,
sugar of virtue under the tongue.

Item: Rec'd this day our poisoned stew
       cooked up by noisy men
       and served in the skulls of the silent.
       Those are stones that were their tongues . . .

*

Staying alive, fear keeps you clean.

I

I see no scarecrows bobbing on the wind
wearing my haggard face.
I feel no weapon closed inside my hand
nagging to be of use.
I ask forgiveness of all the poor and pained
for my unbroken peace,

for my whole luck: that I am fair, but love
all my unlovely friends.
That I am wily and wise enough to save
myself from their bad ends.
That I have never had to swim but live
a dry life on the sands,
facing the tide. That I have peace enough
to sit and watch their disappearing hands.

Some Deaths in the Delta

I

In Itta Bena there was a yearling hog
lived on statistics. A few percentages
made a meal.
It fattened better than anyone had hoped
on its diet of rare slops.
But the day the farmer slashed its throat
that barrel body split its staves
and a family of nine
drowned in the blood of its numbers.

II

The woods' old caves are flattened,
dampness gone back under earth.
A sky away,
pine survivors huddle together,
roots in their hands,
ready for the next step back.

III

The secret ceremony,
old, grave,
warms the darkest room
where the silver lives.
On the eighth day of his life,
swaddled, brown skin, in bridal satin,
the child is held before the man who smiles.
Bloodless, quick,
the whip-sharp knife snaps
and the baby's tongue is out;

ripped off,
gently,
the small simple leaf on its pink stem.
The satin is taken away, the child drifts back to sleep,
naked again.

IV

The fire caught.
A breath of laughter shook the houses
and their meek bones came loose.
Vanished the first day: Sunflower County
and most of Tallahatchie.
Bolivar caught slowly and was holding firm
till it exploded,
and a howl of blood splashed up
and dried like egg on the sky.
Sharkey and Issaquena gave at the center seam
and years of dust flew out,
or ashes.
In Yazoo, when the June fields buckled
everything green went under.

As logic demanded,
it was only the tinder-poor who died in the fire.
But for a week the air was flying bone
and sour tides of smoke.
There was no levee against it.
So the others—
even those who owned the air—

drowned breathing, heads under the wind,
a sack of kittens in the pond.

V

The children who live see clear through the dark.
They hear what silence hears,
and search at ease with their hands.

In the shortest season,
lavender flowers gape from porches,
singing out of the grave.

Mr. Jimmie Washington,
Old Man, Grandfather Turtle

Mr. Jimmie Washington,
old man,
grandfather turtle,
drags his safety down H'way 51.

Nothing escapes him
though he never stops, never looks hard.
(Too many ways into his shell:
Breaking it.
Through the holes
where his cold flesh draws in,
cowers.)

Even when the burning-day comes,
he'll never burn.
That one time, he'll stop in his dim tracks,
meekly, expertly crouch into the dust
and the running fire will pass him by
without a lick,

big dark stone
in the middle of the road.

Highway 51

clover streaks   redder than breath
clover pools   on the long green margins

tiger lilies   children
daisies   swaying wild
queen ann's lace   on knotted roots

blown cotton   something loved
snagged on brambles   in the bomb debris

August is massive   slum whiff
is ardent   the brute sweetness
heavy on the blacktop   weeks dead in the yellow grass

holding us   holding on

English Comp.
(The words are W.W.'s) *

My home town,
is Canton, Mississippi.
It is located in Central Miss., and is said to be
one of her finest shopping centers.
I think you know about this so called friendly town.
When ever I'm comming home
and look at that sign that says "Welcome to FRIENDLY CANTON"
I know that sign was meant for someone
not me.

I was glad when you asked us to write about our home town,
because I want someone else to know of its evils.
This town is so evil
until you can see it in white men's eyes.
It is some men around here that know me
personally that are clansmen,
take for instance the Sheriff,
we been knowing each other every since I was four years old
going to his grocery store with a penny for bubble gum.
Would these men kill me if they got a chance?
I wish I knew the answer.

I will tell you about my people of the town:
My people make the white man treat us
like this.
If any decent white man would ride down North Hickory Street
    on Saturday Night
one could see what I mean.
I will attempt to describe what goes on down this rat hole:

*This was originally an essay by W.W., a freshman at Tougaloo College.

(11)

This place is called the "Hollow"
because it is a narrow street. It (left side) contains a

sandwich shop
cola stand
honky tonk cafe
barber shop
low down blues playing cafe
funeral home
and a fish shop.

On the right side
it is full of
the same thing
mainly
cafes.

The foundation for every sort of disorder
from murder to rape.
People come here (some) for one purpose, that is
to get drunk.
Dressed in overalls, white shirts and red socks.
Some women in after five dresses
loud colors with high heels.
I wont forget the old men either
sitting around the streets eating sardines and crackers
and spitting tobacco juice
in the walking isle.

The thing I hate most is when I see
cops herding Negros into cars.
One night when I was passing through
going home,
two women had gotten to fighting over some man with knives.
One had gotten cut up in the face.

Though it is full of whiskey,
bootleggers,
cuthroats,
clansmen
and what not,
Canton is my home sweet home.
I love it from my heart,
I guess anyone would find faults with
his or her home town.
My mother was born here,
so was I.
There is a spot that I would like to be buried here.
The place has changed a lot,
there used to be trees all up and down the street that I live.
Now there is nothing
but dead roots.
The trees are like the people,
getting old and passing on
like the silent river.
I can remember when I was four years old,
the people I knew were in their prime,
now they are old and grey.
It makes me want to cry by just thinking of them.

Canton is a place full of flowers and flower trees,
if I may say so
it smells as sweet as it looks
in the spring.

1963

Night upon night
clouds swam down the sky
in a black current.
Now I know where the fish hid
live and helpless
going voiceless over the world's edge.

If (people were to say)
the fish had carried flowers
which were (I remember) profuse that year,
and therefore inexpensive;
or something edged with mother-of-pearl;
or perhaps, if nothing frivolous, then
a book; or a reed attesting to
skill at a wind instrument—

but they were themselves,
bare, every third or fourth
lit as if from within,
travelling beneath a streak,
cunning red or silver,
shaped and greased for speed.
Bearing (if anything) something jerry-built
and undeniably personal.

The clouds were fog off the Pacific,
washed up on the sky's far edge.
Painlessly they tore apart,
and they were never less (I remember)
than beautiful.

Now it seems there were fish
chased over the edge; they
had no hands to carry the ransom.
Their scales came down on the underside
of every rain.
When I splashed my feet,
I must have taken them home
in my shoes.

The Cypresses

Highway 61,
Anguilla,
Mississippi

Marooned a million miles, a million years
inland, sun-tortoise crawls this lakebed
dry west, sniffing for the old sea.

The highway
curves,
north

Air tinged green. Always the mad cypresses
are there, sudden, waiting in the river,
drenched to the middle branches. Bare.
Nineteen secret souls of Rolling Fork
huddle in the gnat-stung Yalobusha to
be baptized.

Reverse
curve,
south

The Delta is a moon. It gives no light,
only reflections. Mayersville, Belzoni,
Mound Bayou begin to be invisible. A
faint glow rises from the river, halflight
banks to quarterlight, this chill mist
settling. There are the cypresses,
stripped to the thick dark bone. Arms
upstretched, one by one, they are drowning.

Hearing That My Child's Godmother,
Mrs. Unita Blackwell, Has Lost the
Election for Justice of the Peace,
Beat 4, Issaquena County, Mississippi,
by No More Than Four (4) Votes,
at $10 Apiece,

I Dream for Her

The Mississippi
backs and fills
worse than a stuffed-up drain.
One winterish morning
her Jeremiah in his orange cap
is smiling
like the coach that won the ballgame
from his riverboat kitchen
on the *Mary Jane*
mired between the ditch
and the outhouse.

*

The 59¢ duck she bought
to tickle her god-daughter
comes flapping,
homing for her yard.
It lifts over the long folded hills,
Vicksburg to Yazoo City,
and lands in a green nest,
deep in the kudzu.

The strong weed, thick as cardboard,
swallows the duck's
wool tailfeathers.
She is searching,
calling at it,
flattening the leaves.
She almost steps—
There's the baby
sitting in the kudzu
with its mother's face,
white as the sky.

*

Plums:
where the curve shines
out of the gray
like all kinds of cheeks

*

There is no sheriff.
The phone rings all night.
"No," she says,
"No, that's no job for
a lady."

*

Keys arrive.
They flop through the door—
she's always wanted a mail slot—
and drift up into dunes.
She shovels them under the bed till she's alone.
Back, her hair done,
dressed in her best, what she calls

her "dignity dress,"
she takes an armful.
Keys to files;
to rooms of dirty books at City Hall;
a dozen state capitals
she wouldn't dream of spelling;
the gatekeeper's quarters
at the White House;
Dockery's across town
that won't give credit;
the Issaquena County jail;
a set of real gold car keys
shaped like dice.
They hang from the
cool green necks
of fourteen funeral bouquets.

*

went to sleep
on trumped-up charges

*

Something flaps by,
touches the window.
Jeremiah looks to see
and comes back to bed,
says, "Mrs. Andruss
of the God So Loved The World
Baptist Church
wants your apron
for Sunday service
and says to wish her luck."

Her son is sleeping,
small as he was newborn.
His temperature is down.
A white man is tapping at the door.
She goes through an age,
cloudy, slow,
to answer it.
"What do you want?"
"I'm here for your boy."
"Sleeping."
"Hey, girl,
then get a dog's old front tooth."
So she finds Bo, the neighbor's shepherd
and draws his teeth (foot on his chest),
two to be safe.
"Something from your Mrs. Ainsworth's table."
Harry the gardener
snatches a sleepy, lemony rose for her
right out from under his mistress's blue eye.
She brings a spoon
from the mayor's mirrored silver,
well-water in the spoon.
Finds mushrooms under the pump,
gives him the last of the Johnnie Walker.

"I'm here for your boy."
"Sleeping." Looks at him a long time
her eyes clouding with smoke.
The man is black as a tarred post,

wearing a hat with a tiny peacock feather.
"Take off your hat,
how many times I told you."

Then he is turning, running. "Mama,
I lit the match."
The world book burns,
the doorposts burn,
the old parchesi set they used
when school was out,
and her pussy-willows
pop like corn.
The old white man
is fanning the smoke with his hat.
"Don't worry, girl,
he's safe,
you're welcome, he's safe."
He leads the boy through the rubble.
Barefooted he goes,
hopping.

*

She comes home from a school
she never went to.
She is painting a house,
or she is pasting navy beans
and sea-shells
on a cigar box, making a jewel case.
"Mama,
if I jump in the lake,

will I still be black?"
"Honey, you a peacock!
You got tail feathers!"
Flash frost is coming. She paints
"FOR POTS AND PANS. FOR FABRICS.
DISHES. WALLS."

                    *

She takes two dresses,
some ankle socks,
and her son's geography
for its map of the world,
flat at the poles,
and walks
to the cotton edge of Mayersville.
Says to the first car that stops,
her little brother Freddie at the wheel,
"I'm gone,
don't try and stop me,"
and doesn't look back till they're out of the county.
Half the town is running behind.
She can't hear a word they're saying,
or if they're chasing
or following.

                    *

flower in a field
    redder
            and
                redder

Sugar

in honor of the candidate for Congress from the
Third District of the State of Mississippi

He is a black general now—
never planned to join up but
got drafted
because things rolled the way they did.
Luck!
Baptized in nickel gin,
he reaches through bars of blackness
to pinch the left rear cheek of the world.

His hired men dream of billy clubs,
doing it with gloves on:
The faces on the gauntlet have no blue eyes!
and the river-witness,
silent in the service of all who need,
is glutted with rotten branches,
white and black together, gelded and throttled,
who were poor
in his finicky sight.

Look anywhere but here
for a man
who wants a world of men.
Whose power is his regret of power.
Who would pass it around him,
breaking it like bread on snow,
to startle mouths already open on his name
with bone-sweet choices,
chances,
meaty dreams,
and a little sugar
in this world.

Absolute for Death
for E.K.
Mississippi 1961–1967

Everyone had that moment.
Certain connections burned out,
dangled like shorted wires.
Life at any cost was the last one gone.

Unrancorous, never alone,
they lay down on their hands,
absolute for death,
each behind his own uncrossable line.

Some escaped with half a face
since half was worse than none.
Under the knee caps, gun-butt blows
hacked bone away,
leaving a trick of perfect skin.
Fire ate wood, water ate men.
The old familiar way.
But everything fit then—
deaths echoed and hung in the air
like honest words nearly impossible to say.

The moment had to cool.
Now pain is pain again. Subtraction and division
are all that work.
Survivor's slow, bitter arithmetic.

A Wry Music

Seven are convicted at Meridian

Wind
a wry music
the piney woods give it off like their own
chill
spice

Pelahatchie
      Big Black
          Tishomingo
rivers thick with leaves come moping around the long curves
walking on faces
on long bones
on men's bound ankles narrower than flint

October
cotton-light
Summer lies in drifts
in dunes
high on red wagons
Unwincing light   the shadows of nothing human
pick at it

In a hundred years
one bee
may forgive the worst in us
may stop to drink honey
from a murderer's ear

To a Friend Who Is Leaving Home
to Save Herself From the Sin of Despair

After the talk and anti-talk,
the balancing,
one jumpy foot on the point
where this time meets this place,
you find you've dashed knee-high
into the amber of your choices.

You will live with books and unglazed pottery
in a house the wind dare not touch,
conspicuous among admirers
for what you might have been
were it not for them.
Your children will not chop cotton.

But this island of black soil,
of fierce vines swallowing space,
of mutilating smiles,
good brown-beer wit,
these hundred rusty car-skulls
with poppies in their eyes—

will you dare forgive them
that rawheart morning drowned in snow
when they try to choose you back again?

Alien Corn

to "The Crossroads of the South"

The stones of this city are getting harder.
Bleached flowers in military rows
lean from the clutches of rock-soil.
And you watch for a chance,
with your back-fence eyes,
to plunder me for secrets.

(Well, let me swing my hips
like a simpler woman than I am.
Let me make graceful one- and two-finger gestures
that will be understood internationally.)

Blonde as the grass in January,
walking with legs padlocked above the knee,
she asked, sweet as a lime,
what country was I from.

(I've come to get my hands on your happy endings,
I should have said.
I got this intergalactic glow,
I should have said,
crossing a time-zone.)

Walking your world behind a street map,
missing turns in the dark,
missing home.
Green-stamp Eden,
alien corn sodded for golf,
I thought I could back a hole
in the belly of this stone!

Children of the century,
my old half-brothers,
listen:
The inheritance is yours.
I will study to be an orphan.

Surviving

We fought well together,
in a good rhythm,
taking turns scouting the trail,
plotting our next doomed move,
meeting the enemy breath to breath.
And counting the dead.
Together we pulled their names up over their faces
and spit in the dust, choked on the luck
that anyone survived.
That we survived.
"We will be destroyed!" I'd cry,
thankful for company.

Then one night, coming toward my tent
swinging my lantern, whistling,
my light points to my friend
who drank my whiskey   read my diary   lay in my bed
        wore my clothes
dissolving into the dark
with everything of mine he can drag or carry.

"Friend!" I call. "My friend."
He never stops
but says, to no one,
"I have been destroyed."
He drags my corpse behind him,
bumping across the stones.

A Book of Months

I

Against a forest of leavings.
My hand is closed on the dried cornstalk.
I stand at attention
holding my paper spear.

II

A Mississippi Cypress,
from the kitchen window.
All night it spatters nut-sounds
over the skimpy roof.
Down the road a mile
a hundred ram's horns call us
and call us again.
The heifers begin their howling as soon as the sun goes down.
They live in the dark, in pens,
and fear for their lives.

III

Across the reservoir named for Ross Barnett,
somebody shot at Mr. Winston's daughter's
eye last night,
and shot straight.
She was sitting on a porch like this one,
giving not one blessed thought
to her daddy's politics.

IV

The next-door hogs (in shadow)
churning and pitching
our new spring grass.
That's Sammy who isn't
all there by a longshot
come to take them home,
grunting the words they love him for.

V

M., kneeling
in a swarm of yellow gnats.
Or a thousand flowers.

VI

There's Pat against wild purple,
her back in wisteria.
Eddie dancing to the music,
taking care of business by himself.
Helen in better days,
wide as a full-open flower
about to draw back in.
Me again, already remembering,
already missing them.
The baby's beginning to come clear,
if you look hard,
under my folded arms.

VII

Six Hinds County police cars
blocking the road before it goes
clear out of their grasp.
They are waiting for a killer
or a madman who shook himself
good and loose from Whitfield State,
or a car-thief,
a dumb-ass nigger
who looked crosseyed at a deputy,
or the one Jew too many
for The State.

VIII

The sky is whipped thick. Clouds
group and regroup, coming down dark.
This was the night our first tornado
picked up the other side of town,
ran with it like a football
and fumbled it.
Poor-to-middling whites out there,
living around their first real super-market.
You could hear the roar crosstown—
six hundred boxcars,
all downhill.
I didn't like a single soul
in all South Jackson . . .

IX

How I looked walking the public road,
an eight-month's child
going before me.
Friends warned, lectured,
the logic of the Mississippi male
does not take kindly to a White Girl, Pregnant,
out alone, flaunting,
in this Black town.
They roll their windows down
and speculate.
I walk along the edge of 51,
picking the reddest clover I've ever seen,
daring no one,
eyes down
but open.

X

Dead fall sucks the sky bare.
Slowly it spits back sharp rain.
Good dirt is turned to stone
in the hollow cowfield.
My neighbors' old dark overcoats
inch up the dim side of the road,
and the frozen flag
is snapping at the post-office pole.

XI

Full-face, house.
The evening news (local) lands on the porch.
 (National) floats out through the screen
in Huntleybrinkley's salt-free voice.
They drop into a casual stew—
all together, one square meal
served up at seven, central standard time—
law-breakers, home-breakers, record-breakers,
custom-breakers, ball-breakers.
The faces we know are bloody,
more than likely.
The tall grass you see under the windows:
that soaks up the sound
and holds it down,
dust that it is.

XII

We are leaving.
My face has almost closed back over.
I thought I remembered all my secrets
but this smile that has no corners—
I have to guess—
it is about living out of sight.
Boxes are stacked on the porch
and the door behind me is cracked
on nothing but swept floor.
I am holding the baby,
my hat is slick and yellow
to take the rain.

II.
Brooklyn 11217

Change of Address

I swing out of morning's covers
loose ground moving under me,
a dry tide going out fast
around my ankles.

*

Graffiti still in my head,
paw-prints in my closed palm,
feathers and blood of my first
flight of hard feelings
not yet broken
across fresh paint.

*

Cracking open the rooms,
shaping them to me
    sending my dust messengers
    gluing the new numbers   197   to tongues
    stealing orange sleep on the Chilean rug
    unlocking shutters
    on thumbstained glass

*

Ghosts still visit
at ease here.
They like to tell me how it used to be,
how light and shadow worked these corners,
where green, where yellow were.

My ghost,
dispirited,
tiptoes a thousand miles home

but the cornfield is all paper,
winter-torn,
and remembers no one.

                    *

I am hanging a vial of sparks
slantwise in the doorway,
planting the smooth pit
of the future
under the grass welcome mat.

One day I will wake
knowing
I dream in the language of this house.

In Rooms

I have been alone in rooms,
in houses, even—their doors barricaded
with snow, a month from the news.
Nothing is like it:
Talk and you wonder if that could be a voice.
And you lie lightly, skimming the cream
of sleep off the top of an endless night.

I have been alone in rooms
with cats dozing—their bodies like snakes
coiled around air.
Nothing is like it:
Talk and they hear you and don't hear you.
And you sleep tacitly guarded by their claws,
at the side of their breathing that flows and flows like a river.

I have been alone in rooms
seething with strangers—their presence demanding
my captured presence.
Nothing is like it:
Talk and they blink and answer and do not hear you.
And you see through a film like sleep how you are drifting
into a whirlpool, down, down to yourself.

Who It Is Who Could Not Wait

Off in that other room, sleep,
you hear the faintest jangle—
bottles pushed aside, wind-chimes—
then the bell rips through like light.

At night all phones are answered
in a leap, less than a breath.
Fear snatches half the first ring
and asks in a readied voice

who it is who could not wait,
what news from the unsleeping.
From far off, what surprise strange
as the dream it shook you from?

And it is no one. Hanging
like a curse in its hollow,
silence pulls you in, holds you.
You riffle years of pages,

the closed accounts of friendships,
for one hint of a joker,
and your neck crawls with the cold.
Something like your own guilt then

starts in the motiveless dark.
The click cuts you away, free.
Three o'clock in the dark night
of someone's soul, who had to hear,
shaken, your voice before he slept?

Sunday Morning, Red Hook

Ride out on the sharp hook.
Land that remembers nothing red

      (decades under flowers
      southern cinammon clay
      iron Mars glint)

but Rheingold labels
and easy blood.

Lean on the shipyard fence
held out over greased water.
There. The statue's
stone sober sickeyed face.
Holds of immigrants never guessed
she has her eye on Brooklyn
listing into the bay.

Behind her eye
she dreams of life as a lady good as her name
in the harbor of Atlantis.
   (sea anemone washed close to shore
   pouring deep red and purple dyes against the rock face)

Sunday.
Con Edison frees its flocks.
Loose-feathered soot-birds
nest without singing
in the bitch's spiny halo.

Neighborhood News

NOTICES TO HOME-OWNERS
Plant trees.
For every tree build a fence.
For every fence get a dog.
Let the dog use the fence however he pleases;
you will sleep, free to dream,
your investment protected by trained teeth.
(Consider a second dog for your car.)
You have responsibilities now:
You have bought your island
for $24.99 and a handful of that
dried fish the natives like.
You do not like it,
remember.

NOTICES TO RENTERS
Keep your milk off the windowsills.
Count your kids each night.
The number should be constant or decreasing.
Search their eyes for needle marks.
Stay in the house after dark—there is no
walking without a destination
in a Transitional Neighborhood.
(If you have a car, you may drive it.)
Make small fires, if you wish,

under the stairs, in the bedclothes,
fire being an approved agent of change.
Stay in and watch the pages of the dictionary
projected on your shades,
flowing like a river,
Spanish into English.

NOTICES TO STORE OWNERS

Rinse out the blindfolds that hang like banners
CERVEZA FRIA   OPEN SUNDAYS.
Feed the cat that gritty fish
beached on a rice sack,
feed the mouse that cheese souring on months.
Burn the candles for yourself,
the kindergarten reds   greens   blues
WELCOME HOME   SAFE CROSSING   DEPARTED BELOVED.
You have been notified
in case of emergency.
The A&P is coming with a black glove
on its closed hand.
There will be no clues.
You will be found shaken to death,
your deliberate fingers still on the register keys,
the drawer wide open,
none of your money gone.

With Thanks and Apologies All Around

Marilyn's mother's father
was spared the inconvenience of the Czar's army
by falling from a horse who was glad to oblige,
speaking, as he did, a similar language
at home in Vilna Giberniya.
At home now, the master cynic of Jacksonville, Fla.,
he flays the air beneath his hands
with amiable anger—Bolsheviks, Zionists, Americans,
grandchildren!
Let each spit on the other!

Lucia found the town where her ancestors
still walk to the black oven in the square,
and wash their black clothes between the rocks
when the river is there.
Avigeiano lies like a pebble in a crack
on the margin of her map,
where her homely cousins succeed each other reliably,
choiceless, she says, and free.

Arverna, knowing less, conjectures
her family must have been found, and taken,
among the taller West African tribes,
and has had no instance of dilution,
except among certain cousins,
the Littlejohns, whose noses
keep them from passing.

Our fathers, their fathers,
dragged their futures by the tail
to neutral ground, a hell of questions
others would answer,
and bought admission for a stern price.
With thanks and apologies all around,
we're selling it back at a loss.

The Famous Writers School Opens Its Arms
in the Next Best Thing to Welcome
for A.B.

Good writing, the book tells you,
begins at home.
If it's anything like charity.
Hope for the best, try to relax,
and ignore the spelling.

You are obedient. You write about your kitchen.
"Everything I hate.
It is the place where all the accidents happen."
You are standing at the stove
shaking the saucepan
the way you'd shake a child,
to hurry along the coffee-water.
Oh it is green in here,
the green that punishes public walls,
never the color of leaves or moss
spreading, soft, on the shady side.
The pennies in the linoleum cracks
you're leaving there for luck.
The walls, the floors, the chairs have their flesh scrubbed off,
flayed no-color. All of it shatter-lines,
but holding.

"I think I have something to say,"
you say, separating some of your children,
always tangled up like hair.
Once a year you can expect to disappear

so far down your own throat and belly
a doctor with a miner's lamp
comes looking, calling out names,
some of them yours.
He tells you
you mustn't want to be destroyed
ever again,
admires your youth, your height, your hair,
whatever catches his nearest eye.
But you are the place
where all the accidents happen.
You have a cache of reasons
he isn't going to see.

This morning, though,
with a branch of sunlight
moving against the kitchen window,
words are—cheap?   free?
No. Possible.
In the air.
They blow around
in the wind of your dreams.
"I was dreaming about the word 'surprise'
with a 'z' in it.
Nothing else happened, there was only this word
coming out of my typewriter.
A tickertapeworm, surprizesurprize."

You laugh, slouch a little,
and wait for something surprising to begin.

To saddle the word "surprize"
and ride out the kitchen window forever
over the limp roofs of Brownsville,
across the stone badlands,
Red Hook, Gowanus,
right through the twin castles,
empty purple castles of the Brooklyn Bridge.
Or out to sea past the softening
Staten Island meadows,
dotted with old trees and genuine, pale lakes.

You pour the water
into the Maxwell House,
and turn to the paragraph you've made
with your own limber hands.
You are turning soil,
looking for the place to plant fresh syllables.
The only garden on your block.

Going on Thirty

They still let us in the swamped
doors of the Fillmore
if we have our straight's five.
I'm hunched toward the stage,
a strange tidal bending, and it is
the blackest sea this side
of the moon.
Red lights, buoys stranded,
burn across dead space.
Those are the eyes of undersea gear
that hauls up sound
naked off the ocean floor.

When the waves, blue to purple to good-blood red,
have battered all our ears back into
these sober undefended heads,
the dark comes on again. The lonesome
little eyes stare back. No recognition.
I stiffen for a hard shove,
myself against myself.
Oh I pity me! me! and trust no one,
I who love the stage dead,
nothing begun,
and the dark stalled up there, empty-handed.

Orange Sunshine
for M.P.

He called late
going up in flames
feeling old smashed
glass splinter by splinter
nailing his face
the fire eat him whole
spit him ash
by ash back down

Talk   talk to me through this
sunshine fire I took
I did to my mouth
I'm dead slowly
but if you talk

I chew
an hour to words for him
far away   empty fingered
but I talk
shout   whisper   lie   curse   sing
trying to be cold water
blackish coffee   warm hands
any down thing

I tell him
you're no more
alone tonight
than ever   dear
and you'll be back
in the morning

Wish

never
hid in one
or tossed one through a window
beat with a longhandled spoon on one
or a bow
or a breadknife

sent one through the US mails
never ate one whole
threw a couple in the fire
fished them out squirming

god knows never
curled up to sleep beside one

been chased round corners though
been bitten by them
all my life
and never said no
more   no more
till now

Witness's Report

I saw the cop
thomp your head wide open.
That back seat
is where they keep their dogs
of war.

He's not the first
to empty your slack wits.
The slow bleed
started when your mama's
midwife

tied off the cord,
kissed your wet eyes open
on nothing.
Your mind leaves salty stains:
circles

rank with effort
under your arms; tears of
absolute
stalled motion; blood on toes,
fingers

clawing footholds
on sheer walls others go
around. Who
kicks your head strikes stone now,
layers

of jagged scar,
old ringed tree. He must have
hurt his hands,
the slug-white cop.
While you slumped

maybe thinking
The Lord is my (German)
shepherd: I
want Him on my leash,
he must have bled—so it begins—
for you.

Conference

The President is alone, sitting on his shield, which
looks like a scatter-rug under him. His knees are
pulled up to his chest. He speaks:

In my dreams, the poor came to me
wearing their funny blue hats.
We had all been waltzing, dizzy and sharp
at the party I gave in the tea-rose garden,
and they had groggers,
        monkeys-on-stick,
        and angel cake in five-pound hunks.
They had funny heads
under their hats,
and funny big hands in sleeves like barrels
(I know they were crammed with dixie cups!)
"We're building a house," they told me flat,
"out of left-over root-beer and whistles and cake.
The sweetest old house since the still blew up."
"Watch out for ants!" I said. "Don't sleep.
For rats. For children. For mold on the icing
and spit in the whistles. It happened to me.
Watch out for hunger pangs—don't eat the walls down,
don't don't don't—you'll catch your death!"
"Ah," they smiled. "We've hired an expert.
He's deep. He knows. He says: Step on the ants.
Poison the rats.
Throttle the children.
Spray the icing (or make it plastic—
a good vinyl icing—no one will know.)
And don't get hungry whatever you do."
And they danced away
with their funny blue hearts.

A Fable for Senator Russell

(If we have to start over again)

Sun rose straighter than a jail-bar.
Shone down in everybody's hair,
seeped under collars,
lapped around shoe-tongues.
Everyone carried the drops of gold around
in pocket linings
feeling nearly rich.

(with another Adam and Eve)

Those, who have learned to walk with their palms up,
were arrested for concealing
a dangerous weapon—
body heat,
ropy muscle,
ten good fingernails in a closed hand.

(then I want them to be)

They were bailed out under law
in return for the gold
and the gold feeling,
taken out of the jailhouse shade,
turned three times and aimed

(American)

toward the narrow shop
of the coffin-maker.

The Bedouin Said (When Asked)

"The United States is a land,
always dark and cold and behind the sea.
It is full of beasts."

Yes, grandfather.
And among us a few
whose ruffled fur, as you see, is harrowed away
by our own eye-teeth:

who thought we had learned a redeeming balance
and went forth boldly
on two legs

into a rain of pennies,
not the first of the world's
dumb dancing bears.

Coming to This

My mother's mother
   began her worldly progress
slow as a great ship,
   ballasted with children.
The first to say Ekaterinislav
gave no farewell parades,
   still, she would add,
she studied it from the outskirts long and hard.
At his own intervals, Grandfather sent
money from Baltimore,
   which got them scant
herring and heels of bread.
   Moored in a single place
months at a time,
   Grandmother peddled lace
to ladies, bone buttons to gentlemen,
till, fresh with impatience and some coins,
   again
they'd forge the sea of the continent,
   island to island;
were fruitlessly robbed;
   left the baby buried
in a shroud of yard-end lace
   at a quiet roadside.

It took two years
   and one long lurch of a crossing
to land them here.
   Not strengthened—

pared, whittled to a point, drier than wood,
two sons marooned,
   my grandmother's hair half white.
She slept a full three days
   in her cousin's bed
in Baltimore,
   saying that she could wait
to see the land, whose promises would keep
if they were real. And she awakened
to see them all,
   like cups,
casually broken.

In This Strange Time

In this strange time,

making love under a hush,
nerves filed down,
every move knows it—

someone watching
more than sees.

The baby is dancing between us
in his first strength
and   loving
we make him
   again
       again
          again.

Let Us Open Together
the Last Bud of the Future

"Abramos juntos
el ultimo capullo del futuro."
   (Blas de Otero)

What does it cost?	One finger. Two eyes.
How will I cook with no fire?	Put wing-bones in your shoe, walk them tender.
For wine—	Drink from the breasts of your children.
Will I have fat for my lamp?	From the inside of your thigh. The smoke will be bitter.
Days morning won't come, in the half-light—	Lie in it. Count the hairs on your belly, scratch the number in the dirt and it will come true.
You are boiling the sheets of the sky, the piano keys, the wide red peppers.	Beginning again.
I saw a fox with small fur. He took a guess—	Necklace of foxes, crisp toy feet . . . Just where would you circle?
My good friends see me.	Take these leaves. Tomorrow will be clean, frank, steady. After you pay,
One finger, two eyes. If I don't—	it will belong to you.

III.
Can't Remember
What I Meant by Home

Can't Remember
What I Meant by Home

My room is a brickassed crow's nest. The sea goes almost under me, on wheels. Breaks against the stop sign. Trickles and trickles.

The woman next door, a young woman, throwing bottles at the street. Only her arm pokes out of the high window; no face. She is aiming at her life, hitting windshields, curbstone, the rear bumper of the Ralph Avenue bus, the puny tree that does not shade her house.

The cops are coming to her door, shouldering it till it lets them in. Unshamed, we wait for her to come out covering her face, kicking their navy shins. They do not come and do not come. Then the two big men are closing the door behind them gently, honoring something. One is gingerly on the steps, holding a bowl in front of him. Taking her to the station-house: she the melted candle in the bowl, the soured milk, the blood wrung from a towel. Something spattered from a breaking bottle as it hits concrete. The siren begins again, a long long question. They ride away through a puddle of glass.

Where, on Dean Street, is a cup of sourgrass growing? Bloodroot, trilium, moss in Brooklyn 11217. The saplings are the children of the block association's shy philanderings with a cut-rate Coney Island greenhouse. Such unpassionate wind-abused dry-faced witnesses to an unlucky dream. They live, repeat each other up and down the street, they un-thrive, in one square foot of suffocated grass.

Has any man died on Dean Street hanged? Is there a man here born in a wine cave? Who walked nine miles in snow to the knees, knickered and whistling?

Uncle George takes heights like the Indian he is, glowering over his preposterous stomach, years pregnant with beer cans, tin and all but the flip-top. He says he can walk across the tops of trees, his magic balance erases his weight. Why can't you fly? I want to ask him, I wait for my chance, my tongue mean blue with logic. Because, he tells me one day, leaning across his low gate, you know you shouldn't fly on a full stomach. Want me to fall in the stinking river?

Who loved one woman so hard she broke in two? All the men on Atlantic Avenue, the men on Pacific Street, on State, on Bond, who sit, dogs in the sun, on plastic milk boxes in front of the dusty bodegas—unshaved, noisy, in and out of the windowless steaming poolroom with no sign out front, living on credit, mouths busy with butts, bad Spanish, worse English —all of them (who can say?) claim credit for splintering up one stony woman in their time.

Robberies tend to overtake us, Brooklyn 11217, like certain kinds of weather, between four and seven P.M., weekdays. Christmas is the hard season for purses.

You rent a window and when it stops fogging under your breath, you can watch the garden perform. Brooklyn crouching under the whip of May. At the height of the growing season husks blossom, pods born stark empty. Tea-pink glass shoulders out of the buds, seven-up green at the stem (no deposit no return), sharper than rosethorn. Mojo, the landlord's dog, daydreaming North Parsonsfield, Maine, where he learned the long stride he suppresses like a limp, drops the only thing he can give, his uttermost loving mashed potatoes, steaming against the gate.

Who put his finger on the Bergen Steet trolley track and took it home a penny? Who went to work one day every day, tongue in his pocket? Who didn't? The sun is smarting against the windows as the neighbors file home to nap their dinner down. Light goes out, lights go on, brick and floorboard settle a day closer to the furious smoky collapse, when ah, rooftops will meet gas mains, telephone wires hug around sewer tunnels, and all the cobblestones on Bond Street will dance with exhausted relief. The streets are old, hard-working, scarred underneath many times over, women who've had more children than they needed. The sag, the care-lines, the gaping seams. What a soft heap they will make when they lie down once and for all.

Who caught trolls under the cellar steps and threatened them, in all their old peace (didn't they come with the house, after all, and the century?) with a heavy handful of Bible and a phone call to his priest?

Little bags of soothing fingers move from pocket to pocket, across folded small bills, on any corner. Boys lope away happy, cool, alone, either go home or turn past blind windowboxes, new gas lamps for that oldworld highrent look on YOUR block, past hopeful yellow and green paint jobs over sour barnacled soot, down the realtor's dream block suspended like one good tooth in the mouth of South Brooklyn hung shining between the nerveless rot of neighbor streets. Who wrote on a clean wall nine times,

DOGFACE WORLD   WATCH OUT   ?

Someone's uncle from Brighton Beach drove his taxi up a long hill and down into the river. Up the block, who washes his hands from a teapot outside the door on the day of the funeral, rubbing them shyly together in the ritual of cleansing while a real and muddy rain washes him, staining his gabardine shoulders with metropolitan (20 minutes from Times Square) comfort.

Who sits at my desk, arms on fresh wood sticky with this air, and breathes in the rancid closeness of the bodies of these seasons. The litany says itself. A fist clenched for monday, a crumbling brick, a hump of turd glazed in the heat, the hour. A siren whipping up the wind. Dull untragic thump at the stop sign. Execrations stream off the impact like heat from a wound. Both cars rage away, flinging up pebbles under their rear wheels. Paper bag spilling the wearies, the wednesday brood, where unfresh ladies sunk in support stockings ("no one can tell till the wind blows!") wait for three kinds of buses. Fishbone and sallow eye broken for friday. A small rat, almost friendly he is so small, sleeps his first last hours curled in an open cardboard box on the sidewalk near the PARKALLDAY $3.00. Daisies pretend to be wild clear to the fence of the parlor pentecostal church. The fence holds back a snowfall of paper beating, flapping to get in. Around the corner from the parking meter patrol is called a neighborhood. Alternate side of the street trembling suspended sat. sun. hols.

Lord   Lord   I can't remember what I meant by home